Don't Let Your Insurance Die Before You Do

Randy Christian

This book is dedicated to all the Baby Boomers who bought life insurance to leave to those we will leave behind.

Acknowledgements go to the American College for all the tremendous education provided over the last 30 years in the LUTCF, CLU, ChFC and RICP courses I have taken as I acquired those professional designations, the PACE requirements maintained every year needed to display those designations, and the clients and friend that have trusted me to help guide them financially.

Table of Contents

Intro

Life insurance is important. It can be what makes the difference between a family's staying in their home after a loss and having to leave. It can be the reason that a mother can stay home with the kids instead of having to go back to work. It can be the difference between a comfortable retirement and living hand to mouth. Given that the right kinds of insurance are so important, who am I to be giving you advice?

My name is Randy Christian, and I'm the owner of a company called RChristian Financial Consultants. As a company, we offer financial advice to clients on all kinds of complicated matters. Our job is to make sure that you know what is happening to your money, to explain in easy-to-understand terms what the heck you're doing and where you are going financially, and to take the mystery out of investments, retirement, and, of course, life insurance. Sort of like a financial general practitioner for your financial health.

Personally, I've been in this business for over 31 years, and in 31 years I've seen pretty much everything. I started out as a life insurance agent for The Prudential Insurance Company and worked my way up from there. And let me tell you, the journey wasn't an easy one.

Around 75% of agents failed out in their first year with Mama Pru. And then another 50% failed out in their second year. Fortunately, I was one of the lucky ones, not just because of my skill and long hours of hard work but because I was determined to stick with it! Then came the time to earn professional designations, those snappy little letters that you get to put after your name.

I earned most of my professional designations in the '80s and '90s, when schools were tough. Each course I took meant weeks of studying after I'd finished a long day on the job. And these were real, college-level academic courses, no marketing techniques or the secrets of closing deals here! After all that came the tests, 100 multiple-choice questions deliberately designed to trick you. In short, if you were one of the few who got the 70% passing score on a whopping 13 of these courses, you really knew your stuff!

Now, as the head honcho at RChristian Financial Consultants, I use all those professional designations, plus those 31 years of experience, to make sure that my clients are as financially prepared (and educated) as they can possibly be and to stay on track as changes—some expected and some not so much—occur.

There are tons of different resources for getting financial advice, and you'll learn more about some of them in this book, but what this all comes down to is trust. For the last 31 years, I have been fortunate enough to be trusted by my clients. Trusted to look after their financial futures, trusted to ensure that they and their families will be looked after, trusted to help them make the right decisions. I am a very lucky man.

We often hear "Trust me; I'm a doctor." Well, I'm saying, "Trust me; I'm a financial advisor." It might not have quite the same ring to it, but I'm here to help you. When you finish this book, you should be able to make the right choices when it comes to life insurance, and that, to me, is the reason that I'm here.

So, without further ado, let's get to the heart of the matter, cut through all the technical terminology, and find out just what the heck life insurance is all about.

Boomer's Guide to Life Insurance: How to Get and Keep the Life Insurance You Want

Part One
A Brief Primer of Insurance Products

I'd like you to meet Tom. Tom's a Boomer, just like you and I. He works a white-collar job, likes fishing and cooking out with his wife and kids. He's an all-around great guy and little different from any of us. Back in the '80s, with a new full-time job, a new wife, a new baby, and the thought of others on the way, Tom did the right thing and bought himself some life insurance. Probably a lot like you did. Then, safe in the knowledge that if anything happened to him there'd be money there for his family, and knowing that he'd made a good investment, he went happily on with his life until a couple of days ago. That was when he got the letter....

Now hold up a second here. Before we can get to Tom's problem (which, unknowingly, you might be sharing in), there are a few things that we need to know. Life insurance is a complicated business, mostly because there's plenty of jargon to be thrown around. One of the very first things we need to do is to figure out what kind of life insurance Tom has. There isn't just one kind of insurance, so let's take a few pages to look at the different options. That way, when we circle back to Tom's letter and his problem, we'll have a better understanding of what we're looking at.

Cash Value, Term, Whole Life, Universal Life - All These Terms Make My Head Spin!

All this technical jargon can be off-putting to say the least, but it's not as complicated as you may think. Very basically, there are only two types of insurance: term and permanent. We can break down those categories a little more, but those are the two main kinds. As for cash value, I'm going to ask you to hold your horses on that for a few minutes, but we'll get there!

Term Insurance

Term life insurance does pretty much what it says on the box. You buy a policy for a set term—maybe 10 years, maybe 20 or 30, depending on the policy that you decide to go for. Should you pass away during that term, then the policy will pay out a death benefit to your beneficiaries. If you don't pass away, nobody gets any money (except the life insurance company, of course!). When your term ends, you may or may not have the option of renewing your policy. If you do renew, monthly premiums will be higher than with your original policy, since you'll be older and therefore more of an insurance risk to the insurance company.

Why do people decide to go with term insurance? Generally because it's cheaper—cheaper than permanent insurance, that is. You are also usually guaranteed to convert to a permanent policy with that same company without any medical exam. This is a great option if you later find that you have medical issues that might be a concern for getting a new term policy when the current one runs out. However, the older you get, the more expensive it is to buy a term policy (older people are more of an insurance risk, remember?). And then there's the big downside of term insurance: there's no cash value. We'll get to cash value in a little while, but for now keep in mind that term insurance has no cash value, while permanent insurance generally has cash value.

Permanent Insurance

Permanent insurance is, well, permanent. Or at least it should be. A permanent life insurance policy is designed to cover you for your entire lifetime. Permanent insurance is more expensive than term insurance, but it does have that magical cash value.... Things aren't quite that simple, though, since there are different kinds of permanent insurance. The main two sorts of permanent insurance are whole life and universal life. So what's the difference? Before we can talk about that, we're going to need to take a look at that cash value issue.

Cash Value: What Is It?!

So, the big question: what the heck is cash value? Let's make this simple. Term life insurance has no cash value at all. Permanent life insurance does.

The "cash value" is usually called the "surrender value" or what the insurance company will pay you for surrendering the contract and relieving them of their legal and binding obligations to you. These obligations are such things as future growth of the cash value, the tax-free death benefit, and other contractual benefits. Point in fact: other than permanent life insurance products and annuities, there are no other insurance contracts that have "cash value" or "surrender value." Your auto policy can be paid for 20 years and when you cancel it, the policy is not worth anything. It's the same with term insurance. The "cash value" gives the permanent life insurance policy itself dollar value. Also, except for bank statements and investment account statements, there are no other products that state the current value—houses, cars, precious metals, and land all have market value, which is not known until there are a buyer and seller and the deal is done.

When you have a permanent life policy, you pay a monthly premium. You might actually pay annually, but let's stick with monthly to keep things simple. An overly simplistic way of looking at how this works is as follows (mind you, this is greatly simplified for this book, and any highly educated professional will argue the finer points of this statement, but then, this is for those of us who buy this stuff and use it, not those academians who design and study it!): Your insurance company divides that premium into two (not necessarily equal) parts: costs and saved. The cost part of the money will be paid to the insurance company since they are in business to make money (duh!), with some of those dollars invested in reserves so they can pay all the claims if you pass away or cash in the contract. As the contract ages and, depending on the finer details, the cash value increases, well, what happens to it depends on the kind of policy you get, but we'll get to that in a moment. Basically, the cash value is like money in the bank. In some policies it collects interest;

in others it's invested in the various investment products. You can borrow against it. It might go towards your death benefit if you die, but in some cases it doesn't. If you cancel your policy, you will get that cash value back (often minus some fees). You might be able to "withdraw" that money. Need a down payment for your vacation house? Bingo! Borrow some of that money in your insurance policy. Need money for retirement? Again, there's that cash sitting in your insurance policy. That saved portion is your cash value.

A permanent insurance policy has a cash value AND a face value. Term insurance only has a face value. The face value is the amount of the coverage of your policy. So you might have a policy that pays out $200,000 if you pass away, so the face value of your policy is $200,000. Ideally, every time you're paying premiums, you're adding to the cash value of your policy! That's how it's *supposed* to work, but not so much sometimes, as we'll hear more about later.

All of this means that you can look at life insurance like a house. Term insurance is like renting a house. You pay rent, and you have a place to live. Permanent insurance is like buying a house. You pay the mortgage, but you're also building equity since you have ownership. You're putting money towards buying the house, just as you put money towards your cash value. With that said, let's go back to looking at those different kinds of permanent insurance policies.

Types of Permanent Insurance: Traditional Whole Life vs. Universal Life

The real difference between whole life and universal life permanent insurance lies in how flexible they are. You're going to want to hold onto your hats for a moment here, because we're going to get a little technical!

Whole Life Permanent Insurance

Okay, quick recap here. Permanent life insurance: you pay premiums, and it builds a cash value. The costs are built in. Remember all that? Whole life insurance is the simplest option, and it does exactly what you've just learned about permanent insurance. If life insurance was a "buy and hold" with no management decisions to make, it would be whole life. There are two kinds of whole life policies, though, and they depend on what kind of life insurance company you choose.

- **Participating Whole Life**: These whole life policies come from mutual life insurance companies. That means that the company is owned by the people who own the policies and participate in the profits of the company when the company pays a dividend. Neat, right? In this case, you may get dividends each year if the company makes a profit, just like if you held stock in the company, except that the dividends are not taxed. Mutual life insurance companies have been in business for a long time and often "count on" the dividend payments and project them into the future of the policy performance. These companies are not traded on the stock market, so they are seen as being more stable. The value of the company doesn't depend on the stock market. But that also means that a mutual life insurance company only has as much money as its customers pay; it can't get more money through issuing new stock on the stock market.

- **Stock Whole Life or Non-Participating**: Stock whole life policies come from publicly traded insurance companies— that is, companies that are traded on the stock market. They pay dividends to the stockholders not the policyholders. That means that the company is seen as a little less stable, since its worth and its "rating" (how reliable a company is seen to be on the financial market) are based on how well it is performing on the stock market (as well as on the economic climate as a whole). On the good side, though, publicly traded companies tend to have easier access to money to grow the company since they can issue stock to raise money.

The ins and outs here aren't terribly important. What is important is that you realize that the difference between a participating and a non-participating insurance company is the dividends. Mutual company (participating) whole life pays tax-free dividends to the policyholders, and stock company (non-participating) whole life doesn't. Mutual companies are less likely to be affected by changes in the stock market or the economic climate in general. If you get a $300,000 policy, you will get that money. That's an important point to remember as we get into universal life. Whole life is generally the most expensive type, all other things being equal, because all the risk is on the insurance company.

Universal Life Permanent Insurance

Universal life insurance is technically known as flexible premium adjustable life insurance. In basic terms, it offers you more flexibility than a whole life policy. With a universal life policy, you can change the amount of coverage you have, change the premium payments, and generally decide how much money you spend. They all have withdrawal and loan features, and most (though not all) have a schedule of surrender charges or surrender penalties for many years (up to 15 or 20!) that will limit when and how much of your cash value you have access to. Having a great year? Then put more money into your life insurance! Bought a house this year? Then put a little less into your policy.

There's another difference too: with a universal policy, you can use the interest that your saved money gathers to pay premiums. That means that, once you have a certain amount of cash value, you might not need to pay premiums at all; the policy might start paying itself. (Don't try this trick at home without professional advice!) We might run into a problem there, which we'll discuss later, but for now, that seems like a pretty good benefit! There are three kinds of universal life insurance, and the difference between them lies in how your cash value is used. Universal life insurance works exactly how you've just learned. Lots of flexibility!

- **Traditional Universal Life:** Traditional has interest rates tied to the interest rate part of the economy. It has a minimum guaranteed rate, determined when issued and in the contract, and a current rate of interest, determined by the economic environment. The cash value is guaranteed by the insurance company. And the interest earned by your cash value (which is a rate set by the insurance company monthly and is based on current interest rates) can later be used to pay premiums. You can adjust your insurance to meet your changing needs over time, making this a convenient option.

- **Variable Universal Life:** These became popular in the late 1990's when the stock market was doing so well during the dot-com boom (just before the dot-com bust!). With a variable universal life policy, you get all the flexibility of a universal policy with one big difference: the money that is saved (your cash value) is invested in the stock market through "investment subaccounts." So, unlike the traditional policy above, there are often little guarantees on the cash value. Also, the expenses are pretty high, ranging as much as 3-5% per year. Your life insurance company will have a portfolio of companies you choose to invest in, and your money will be invested with these. You'll be asked about the level of risk you're prepared to take (higher risk meaning the possibility of making more profit) and what your investment goals are to help you and the agent decide which options are best for you. You usually will be able to move money around between investments too. Thus, the value of the investments is what determines the cash value of the policy: If the investments go up, that's great! If the investments go down, not so much! However, the fees and expenses are deducted from the cash value and your premium payments regardless of the investment performance, which is risk that the owner agreed to when he bought it.

- **Indexed Universal Life:** An indexed universal life policy is a bit of a compromise. You get the best of both worlds here! In this case, your cash value isn't directly invested in the market, so there is no loss of principal risk like with the variable policy. Instead, it is "linked" to a financial index, maybe the Dow Jones or the S&P 500; the index depends on which life insurance company you choose. Your cash value will grow as the index it's linked to grows. And the interest it earns is credited to the cash value like with the traditional policy. The potential rates are usually much better than the traditional's. If the index falls instead? Your policy will guarantee your cash value. There is less investment risk here than the variable, better potential interest rates than the traditional, and lower fees than the variable.

Back to the Problem...

Now that we're all up on our life insurance lingo, let's get back to Tom and his letter. Tom, with all his great intentions, did what most of us did back in the mid '80s and bought himself a solid insurance policy from a well-known, big, old insurance company, which he then promptly forgot about. Well, "forgot" might be a strong word. He knew, in the back of his mind, that the policy was there, that it was a good investment and a security blanket, and was counting on the fact that it would always be there. He had, after all, bought a permanent policy, and that's what permanent means, right? As we're about to see, many life insurance policies have a problem that many Boomer policy buyers—and, in fairness, the well-intentioned salesmen—never foresaw. And Tom's about to learn this the hard way....

Part Two
The Boomer Retirement Plan and Life Insurance

So, sitting at the breakfast table one morning, Tom opens his fateful letter and reads it. When he's done, he reads it again, a puzzled look on his face.

"What's that?" asks Mary, Tom's wife, putting a fresh cup of coffee down in front of him.

"A letter from the insurance company," says Tom, frowning.

"And?" she prompts, half showing interest and half keeping an eye on the eggs on the stove.

"Er ... it says that our life insurance policy is underfunded and that it's about to run out," Tom says, scanning through the letter one more time.

Mary snorts a laugh. It's tough to make her really laugh at this time in the morning; she's never been what you'd call a morning person. "That's ridiculous," she says, scooping eggs out of the pan. "It's permanent life insurance—it can't run out. The computer printout showed it growing until age 95 or 100. That's what ... what's his name? The agent said. When did we get this? After the dot-com bust? About 2001? Anyway, they probably just made a mistake."

"I guess," says Tom, shrugging and folding the letter back into its envelope. Mary is probably right; permanent insurance is permanent, and it can't run out, he reasons. But something niggles, and he decides that he'd better call the life insurance company after breakfast and get all this cleared up.

Do You Know Where Your Policy Sits?

In the old days, we used to buy ourselves a little insurance policy from an insurance agent who worked for the insurance company, and then forget about it, knowing that the agent would take care of things, and the company and the agent would let us know if decisions needed to be made. Now, I'm going to tell you something that you might not want to hear: for the most part, those days are over. There are still good agents who service their clients, but too often, not so much. There are a couple of reasons for this.

The first reason is because the nature of the life insurance industry and how policies are sold has changed. Insurance companies do still have agents, but over the last 10-20 years, we've seen independent insurance agents, people who aren't attached to just one insurance company. In a way, that's a good thing, because it means that you get more choice. Insurance shopping is easier if you can go to one guy who can tell you about policies from several different companies, right? On the other hand, this also means that there's no one there to take care of that policy once you've bought it. The independent insurance agent, just like the company agent, focuses on selling you a policy. But once you've got that policy, he's most likely not going to take care of it for you, because his living is from new sales, not service of existing policies. The insurance industry has increased the commissions for new sales and reduced the "residual commissions." This incentivizes the good agent to sell rather than to service.

Which brings us to the second reason. Remember all that stuff we learned about insurance policies earlier? In the past, most people owned whole life from a mutual insurance company, which is what I refer to as "buy and hold." You didn't need to do anything, just pay your premiums and get on with life. But this is no longer true. For reasons that we'll get into in a little while, many of us Boomers have universal life and universal variable life insurance, or some form of it. Now, remember that a part of a variable policy is going to be invested. Can you see why it might be a problem if the insurance agent isn't watching your policy? Investments are a risky business;

they need changing and observing, and the stock market is pretty fickle these days. If the insurance agent isn't going to be watching your policy, then who is?

Unfortunately, there are a whole lot of people like Tom who are suddenly finding out that their life insurance policy might not be exactly what they thought, and might not be performing in a way they'd like. And that's why it's important to find out exactly where your policy sits.

How do you find out what's going on with your life insurance policy? Well, ideally, you hire a financial advisor to review your policy for you. But we'll get to all that a little later. In the meantime, why don't we find out exactly what's going on with Tom's policy?

But I Bought Permanent Life Insurance!

Breakfast digesting, Tom goes into his office and looks up the number for his insurance company to give them a call. He wades through the customary automated menu until he's finally talking to a real, live person. Then he explains the problem.

"Just a moment, sir," says the young-sounding man on the other end of the phone.

Tom can hear the clicking of computer keys. He sits back in his chair, looking out of the window and wondering if the weather will hold. If it does, he might set up the grill in the yard this afternoon.

"Here we are, sir." The voice on the end of the line comes back. "I've checked your account, and the cash value on that letter is correct. And given the current cost of insurance and the assumed rate of return, the policy will expire in 12 years. Yes, that is correct. Would you like to know the current market value of the subaccounts? Shall I connect you to someone who can better explain the issue to you?"

His heart speeds up, and Tom takes a few deep breaths before answering. "Yes," he says curtly.

He's mad. But he doesn't want to blame this young man, and he's determined to hold onto his temper until he's got a decent understanding of what's going on.

Ten minutes later, he's even madder and no closer to understanding what's happened to his permanent life insurance policy. Through all the technical talk and jargon, only one thing has become clear: he's got to pay the insurance company a solid chunk of cash or let his insurance policy lapse, since it is effectively worthless. Slamming the phone down, Tom puts his head in his hands and wonders how he's going to explain all this to Mary.

Help! My Life Insurance is Running Out!

Let's see if we can unravel exactly what's happened here. How on Earth can a permanent life insurance policy run out? Surely that's contrary to the very definition of permanent? In order to understand this, we're going to need to step back in time a little bit....

The 1980s. Big hair, loud music, and lots of money. Remember those days? Michael Douglas on Wall Street, walking around with that huge mobile phone? Those were the days when most of us Boomers bought our life insurance policies. And like our parents before us, we signed on the dotted line, locked our policies away, and went on our merry way, confident that we had a solid long-term life insurance policy.

Not so fast... There's a problem here. Most of our parents had mutual company whole life insurance, but things aren't as simple as they were back in the old days, because of those fancy new universal life insurance policies. Why? Well, that gets a bit complicated, but we've got all our life insurance jargon down, so you should be able to handle it now!

The Beginnings of Universal Life Policies

In the late 1970s up until the mid '80s, interest rates were high, well into the double digits. The stock market was booming, and people everywhere were making money. This gave life insurance companies an idea: use the great economy, awesome interest rates, and high performing stock market to earn themselves some money and get their clients more money. And so, universal life insurance policies were born (the ones with the investment component, remember?).

The idea was that part of your money would be invested in the stock market or tied to current interest rates in some form or another, taking advantage of the good economic climate. This gave you the chance to earn more cash value for your policy faster than by other means. But there was a trade-off: while with an old style life insurance policy, your monthly premiums would be constant and wouldn't change over time, with these new universal policies, your monthly premiums could get more expensive the older you got. There is a risk that at the time didn't seem a big one, but has come back to bite us. That seemed fairly reasonable: after all, you pose more of an insurance risk the older you get, and it costs more to actually insure you as you get older. Still, though, that rise in premiums made some people uncomfortable. But life insurance companies were quick to explain that the extra cost over time really shouldn't be a problem. Why? Because the money you were going to make through investments and/or high interest rates was going to be more than enough to cover the extra costs. Not only that, but with the economy booming, the money you were going to make on investments was going to be more than enough to cover the extra costs of more expensive premiums AND increase your cash value. So, really, there was nothing to worry about.

Most Boomers looked at the numbers, nodded, and signed on the dotted line. The projected growth of these new universal policies was very tempting. We all looked around and saw the excesses of Wall Street and thought, hey, why not? Why shouldn't we profit from that too? Times were good, and these policies promised us a very healthy retirement fund when we needed it.

Where Things Go Wrong

Let's rephrase that last sentence: Times were good, and these policies promised us a very healthy retirement fund *if they performed as they were forecasted to perform*. And now maybe you're starting to guess where things went wrong. Actually, there were two problems.

The first of these problems is pretty obvious. The economy tanked. Those high interest rates and stellar-performing stocks didn't last. There was that dot-com bubble in 2001. Then everything crashed in 2008. We all are well aware of the fact that the economy is not performing as it did back in the 1980s and '90s. In turn, that means that the investments made through your universal and variable life insurance policy also didn't perform well. Your policy didn't make as much money as you and the life insurance company thought it would.

You still might not think that that's a big problem. After all, you paid your premiums, your policy has cash value, and it's designed to protect you for your entire life. Okay, you didn't make as much money from investments as you thought you were going to, but still, it wasn't like you'd just invested your own money and lost it, right? Um ... let's get to the second problem and see where that takes us.

The second problem is that, for the most part, we didn't read the fine print when we bought the policy. And, quite probably, we didn't keep an eye on that policy to see how it was performing or changing over time, which might have given us a clue that something was going wrong. Tom definitely didn't, or he wouldn't have been so taken by surprise by his letter.

You see, hidden inside those life insurance policies that we so carefully signed but maybe didn't quite read all the way through (and, to be fair, the policies are complicated, loaded with legalese, and not easy to read in the slightest) was something that changes everything. The design of the policy is that the premiums go in, the insurance company takes its expenses and costs and fees, and the money earns interest, sometimes through subaccounts, and then pays for the cost of the insurance from the cash value.

Get that? If your investments don't perform well enough to cover the costs, the insurance company sends a letter to advise you that more money is needed to cover the costs or the policy will expire, *as per the terms of the contract.* In fact, they can withdraw money right up until your cash value is zero. Life insurance into your later years? Nada! That little nest egg, that retirement plan, that down payment for your vacation cottage? Gone!

Where has it gone? It's gone to pay for your insurance. You've been getting older, and as you've been getting older, it's been costing more and more to keep you insured. When you bought your policy, you were told what the minimum premium payment was, and you paid it. You kept paying it. Sadly, over time, as the cost of insuring you went up and the actual amount of interest or investment decreased, the minimum premium was no longer enough to cover what was needed to insure you, and what was earned by investments in a poor financial climate wasn't enough to make up the difference. So, instead, the insurance company began taking money out of your cash value to cover the costs. And now that money's all been spent, and there's a problem. You're underfunded.

And when the cash value is gone? You've got two choices. You can either let the policy expire, since it's worthless, or you can pay the insurance company a bunch of money to make up the difference yourself.

How This Happens

To make things a little clearer, let's look at a quick example. We'll choose Tom, since we already know him.

In 1990, when Tom bought his policy, he was young, only in his early 30s. That meant he was pretty cheap to insure. After all, he was healthy, fit, and a very low risk. He didn't even smoke! He opted for a policy with a $200,000 death benefit, a universal variable policy, as it happens. He kept up the minimum premium payments and paid the same amount every year.

At the beginning, this was fine. The cost of actually insuring Tom was pretty low, so most of his minimum premium payments went into that cash value portion of his policy, which was invested. But as Tom got older, the cost of actually insuring him went up. By the time he was in his 50s, and had already had a minor heart attack, the cost of actually insuring him was increasing. And the market went through the boom/bust of the dot-com affair and again through the recession of 2008-09. But Tom was still only paying the minimum. He looked at the statements he got every now and then and didn't really understand them, but they showed he had the insurance, and the cash value looked okay, so he figured he was okay.

Theoretically, this wasn't a problem. Those investments were supposed to cover all the extra payments, remember? But with his investments doing badly, and his insurance company's needing higher costs of insurance every year to actually insure him, they began to take that money out of his cash value account. They did this until eventually they didn't have enough to cover the costs of the policy. Which was when they sent him a letter telling him his policy was underfunded.

Tom's choice is to either let the policy go, or pay the insurance company the much higher premium needed to actually insure him now that he's older and cover the future costs. And that's just for starters. If he decides to pay these costs, then he can keep his insurance policy. However, he's going to need to start paying a much higher set of premiums each year to make sure that the cost of actually insuring him is covered. And if he wants to rebuild that cash value? Then he's going to have to pay even more in premiums to ensure that his actual insurance is covered and that there's enough left over to add to his cash value account.

And that, my friends, is how a permanent universal variable life insurance policy can run out. And it's exactly what has happened to Tom, as he finds out the next day when he meets with a financial advisor who explains all of this to him.

The bottom line in all of this is that:

- It is possible for a permanent life insurance policy to "expire," which is referred to as being "underfunded."
- Once your policy reaches this point at the extreme, you're between a rock and a hard place, since you either pay a large sum of money to keep the policy going or write off the policy (and all the money you've paid into it) completely.
- Caught early enough, it can be easily and affordably prevented. The only way you can know if this is happening to you is to review your life insurance policy and find out what's going on!

Let's repeat that last one: the only way you can know if this is happening is to review your life insurance policy. Hold on. That implies that there are options here. And you're right. All is not yet lost!

What's Tom's Plan?

Let's take a second to check back in with Tom and see how he's doing. He's been lucky enough to find a good financial advisor, who's explained to him clearly what has happened and outlined his options.

"So, what are we going to do?" asks Mary. She looks worried and has the little lines she gets around her eyes when she's tired.

"Well," Tom says slowly, "we're in a tough spot, and there's a couple of good options that we need to think about."

"Which are?" She seems more hopeful now, since Tom does too.

"We can always let the existing policy lapse, and instead get a completely new policy," Tom answers.

Mary looks confused. "But we're both pushing 60. Come on, aren't we a bit old to be life insurance shopping?"

Tom laughs. "Not according to this guy we're not. He says that that's one possibility, and we could switch companies. But..."

"I like the but," says Mary. "But what?"

"Well, the insurance company we're with is in good shape. It's got a good rating, and performance has been improving. The advisor seems to think we could decrease the death benefit a little, increase the premiums we pay a little, and then continue with the policy we have. There's still some cash value there, which we could add to if we lower coverage and increase premiums. We've got that CD that's paying a whopping .5%, and we can dump that in to help get back on track. The surrender charges are low, so if we need it, we have access to it. He is willing to help manage the investment for us for a small fee. "

Mary thinks for a minute. "No more medical exams?"

"Not if we stick with the company we're with."

Tom and Mary need to think about this for a while. But the important thing is: they have options.

I'm Not Sure I Have Enough, But Am I Too Old to Have Options?

We'll answer that question right off the bat to stop you from worrying: no, you're not too old. You have options. There are things you can do that will stop your permanent life insurance from running out or becoming underfunded and stop you from losing your entire nest egg. The first and most important thing that needs to be done is to review your insurance policy to see where it's at right now and what the current conditions will project into the future. There are people who can help you do this, and we'll discuss your options when it comes to that later. But for now, the important (and good) news is that there are things that can be done. A good financial advisor can help you review and possibly even change your policy to reflect what you want and need, preferably **before** your policy reaches the point of Tom's and is underfunded. Reviewing your policy annually will basically give you one of three results.

1. All's Well

The first, and obviously preferable, result is that your life insurance policy is absolutely fine. It's performing as it should, getting the kind of results you need and can expect, and all's well. Don't sit too comfortably, though. The financial market changes often and quickly, so even if your life insurance policy is doing well, you should still go through the review process every couple of years to make sure everything is still up to scratch. The traditional universal policy is tied to interest rates, and as we all know, interest rates have been close to 0 for several years. While these policies have minimum rate guarantees, the performance needs to be checked. Obviously, the variable policy needs to be monitored more frequently, since the cash value is in the stock market.

2. Your Policy Needs Tweaking

The second possible result that could come from an insurance policy review is that, while your insurance company is sound and reliable, your policy itself isn't doing quite as well as it should be. This isn't a disaster, since in most cases a policy can be what I like to call "tweaked." There are three main ways your existing life insurance policy can be tweaked to make it better, by which I mean more secure for the future and either earning more for you or losing less for you.

i.   You can increase the premiums you pay, since this will put more money toward covering the cost to actually insure you. This can help to build the cash value and have more earning interest.

ii. You can decrease the death benefit. If you lower the amount of money your policy gives out in the event of death, you lower the cost of actually insuring you. This allows the cash value to grow better.

iii. A combination of both of the above.

Tweaking an existing policy is often the best solution for most people. Why? Because you stay with your policy and company, which means that you won't need to have another medical exam. Insurance medicals are time consuming, and there's always the risk that the exam will show something that makes you more of a risk, more expensive to insure, and therefore means paying more to be insured (or the worst case scenario being uninsurable, meaning you're such a big risk that the insurance company refuses to sell you a policy). That means that tweaking your current policy is preferable over getting a new one.

3. A New Policy

Finally, your insurance policy review could show that your policy just isn't performing well at all. Or even, in some cases, that the insurance company itself isn't performing well at all, and the company isn't willing, after requesting a re-rate due to improved medical conditions, to lower the cost (i.e.: standard to preferred or a higher-than-standard rate due to a medical condition at the time of purchase to a standard rate now since the condition has been successfully treated). Maybe the rating of the insurance company has been lowered, for example. Or there's some combination of issues that simply makes moving to another company's product the better solution. In these cases, a whole new policy is required. That might mean a move to another insurance company.

For example, you might want to take that cash value out of your existing policy and put it in another policy that will provide better or more benefits than the current policy. If, after a discussion with a financial advisor, you decide that your policy is no longer needed (maybe you own your home outright, the kids have finished college, etc.), you might decide to surrender your policy completely and use the cash you've gathered elsewhere or sell it on the secondary market for a higher amount than the cash surrender value. Or, in some cases, exchange it for a paid-up policy. This is sort of a compromise: you have a modest amount of life insurance, with some cash value but no premiums to pay. But these are your three basic options if you're afraid that you don't have enough life insurance, or that you're at risk of your policy's expiring before you do, due to these performance and funding issues.

How Old is Too Old?!

In the interests of full disclosure, I have to say that yes, there comes a point where it's not worth buying a new policy. For example, a 75-year-old man who wants a new policy for $50,000 of coverage. His premiums work out to $7000 a year. That means that he only has to live another seven years and he'll have paid almost his entire coverage amount in premiums. As long as that 75-year-old is healthy and can reasonably expect to live that long, no, that insurance policy is not a sound financial decision.

However, what all this comes down to is that there is no one-size-fits-all option when it comes to life insurance. Everyone has different needs. Depending on your values, health, age, overall financial situation, family, and a whole bunch of other things, the right policy for you will be different. That's really why it's important that you find out about the options.

The truth of the matter is that we Boomers are a healthy lot. We're expected to live for a good, long time and to have a relatively good standard of health. Is 60 too old to get a new policy? To make changes to your existing policy? Well, how much longer do you expect to be around for? For many of us, no, 60 really isn't too old. When it comes to insurance, yes, the sooner (or younger) you buy, the better. But that doesn't mean that it's not worth getting a new policy or changing a policy once you're of a certain age.

I Have Some Term Insurance. Should I Convert it to Permanent?

All of this bad news has so far been about permanent life insurance, and that might have you thinking that it could be best to skip permanent life insurance completely. Why not just stick to term insurance? That way, none of this bad stuff can happen to you, right? As fate would have it, Tom got into a very similar conversation later that same afternoon when he was playing golf with his buddy John.

"So, that's pretty much what happened," says Tom, after outlining his life insurance disaster.

John sucks his teeth and shakes his head. "I'm sorry. I wish there was something I could do."

"We're looking into it. We have some options and are glad we got real advice and not a sales pitch," Tom says.

John loads his clubs into the back of the cart, and the two hop on for the ride to the next hole.

"Strange, though," says John, navigating his way down the path. "I've been thinking about life insurance too over the last couple of weeks."

"Mmm?"

"Thing is," John says, steering carefully, "I got term insurance, and it's about to expire. Expires in a couple of months, actually. The term's up. So I've been wondering what to do about it. I mean, I looked into the options. But, man, this is pricey stuff we're talking about here."

"Pricey how?" asks Tom, curious to see if John's uncovered some options that he hasn't.

"Well, I got a choice. I could renew the term insurance, but they're quoting me a premium that's more than double what I was paying before. Or I could switch to a permanent policy. But then the premiums are even more."

Tom nods as John brings the cart to a halt. "Thing is, insurance is a sort of investment—both the cash value and, more importantly, the benefit that my wife gets when I pass," he says, hopping out.

"I get that," John says, jumping out too. "But with everything you've just said about your problems, I'm starting to think that going with term might be my best option. It's cheaper anyway."

Tom thinks about this as they play the hole. It's a fair point, he guesses, since he's still stinging from the shock of his insurance issue. He's lost a fair amount of money, after all. But then, would he change his policy from permanent to term? In the long run, he thinks, no, he probably wouldn't.

But Why Not Switch?

Should you change that term insurance to permanent insurance? After all the bad news I've given you about permanent insurance, I'm still going to say yes. And I'm going to tell you why.

The primary reason that I would always encourage you to go with permanent insurance is that the reason we buy life insurance is because we love those we would leave behind. The industry has gotten off track with such a focus on the cash value, which certainly is an essential part of the permanent policy value. But the reason for permanent life insurance is to have it in force *when you die!* Make no mistake—the mechanics of the policy, the savings and investment of the cash value, are important financial concerns and should be properly managed, but the reason for having permanent life insurance is to assure that the policy will be there in your old age. Term can't do that, and investments might or might not still be there. (That's a subject of a future book!) Let's have a quick summary of three basic concepts to help me explain myself: term & permanent (whole life and universal).

Term

Okay, term insurance is cheaper; that's a pro. But term insurance has no cash value. You put money into your policy, but (unless you die before the term is up and your family collects the benefit) you don't get anything out, which is a serious con.

Whole Life

Whole life insurance is permanent, and it has cash value, both of which are good. The cash value is guaranteed by the insurance company, something that's both good and bad. On the good side, that means there's very low risk. On the bad side, that means that your cash value might not grow as fast as it potentially can with a universal life policy.

Universal Life

Again, universal life insurance is intended to be permanent and has cash value. There's that investment part, though. On one hand, that means you can potentially make more money and grow your cash value more quickly than with whole life. On the other hand, it means you're taking more risk and will have to be careful to watch your policy to make sure it's performing properly.

I compared life insurance to a house earlier, and that analogy still stands. The death benefit is the shelter. Term insurance might be cheaper, but you're only paying rent. You'll pay rent every month until your landlord decides to throw you out (or you want to move), and when you walk out of the door of that house, what do you have? Nothing. With permanent life insurance, either whole life or universal life, it's more like paying a mortgage. You're still paying every month, probably more money than you would pay in rent, but at the end of the day, when you decide to move, you can sell that house. Sure, you might not get 100% of the money (unless you've already paid off that mortgage), but you'll get some of the money. All in all, you're in a better position if you decided to buy a house, right? All in all, you're in a better position if you decided to get permanent insurance. Because you have equity and the potential of keeping it until you die in your old age.

Whether to go for whole life or universal life insurance is a different issue, one that depends a lot on how much money you have, how much risk you can afford to take, how old you are, and what your investment goals and plans are. But I think we can agree that whichever option you choose, you'll end up in a better position than you would if you had bought term insurance. Tom's buddy John is a great example of this. He bought term insurance, and it's about to run out. He's spent the last 29 years paying premiums on that insurance policy. Sure, if he'd passed away, his wife and daughters would have been provided for. But he didn't. And now he's in the position of having paid all those premiums and having nothing to show for it. He's basically back at square one, shopping for a new insurance policy, and all the money he's spent on his old term policy is gone with the wind. And starting over means a new medical exam and higher cost since he's older.

But there's an additional reason that I would encourage anyone to get permanent insurance if possible: the insurance market has changed. The problems we're talking about here tend to affect us Boomers because we all bought similar kinds of policies over the last 10-20 years. The insurance market moves fast, and that means that there are now more options than ever before. Some of these changes are social: health care has improved, life expectancy has increased, underwriting has improved, and the pure cost has declined. Insurance is cheaper than before. But policies themselves have also improved, as have life insurance companies as a whole. There are policies that give coverage for critical illness, chronic illness, and terminal illness; and some have retirement income benefits and lower costs due to longer lifespans. There are new policies that include other investment options, such as the "fixed index universal life." You have choices, and it would be foolish not to consider these into the equation.

Just one example: permanent life insurance policies have changed a lot in recent years in terms of age. It used to be that a permanent life policy matured at the age of 100. When a policy matures, it means that the cash value is equal to the face value. At that point, why pay more premiums since you can't add anything to the policy? Nowadays, it's much more common for a policy to mature at the age of 120, and some policies even continue until "the death of the insured." This has happened for a number of reasons, not least because we're all living longer than ever before. And that's only one way in which permanent life insurance has changed in the last couple of decades. The market is now a lot different than it was 30 years or so ago when we Boomers were all life-insurance shopping for the first time.

Bottom line? Permanent life insurance products are great products. They are assets. And like any other assets, they need to be managed and watched over. But they're still assets, which is a lot more than can be said for term insurance. If you have the means, consider converting that term policy to permanent!

What about John?

Tom, being the good friend he is, passed along his financial advisor's number to John, who immediately made an appointment. After reviewing all the info and explaining matters to John, the advisor eventually helped him decide to switch that term insurance to permanent. Luckily, this was quite easy to do, since John's term insurance policy, like most term insurance policies, allowed him to convert to a permanent policy with the same company without having to undergo another insurance medical exam. Now John's paying more in monthly premiums, but he's building equity as well and will be able to keep the policy until age 120 (which is plenty long enough!). And that sounds like a sound financial decision to me!

The Meat of the Matter

What's our take-home message here? There are two facts I want you to know about life insurance, facts that I think everyone should know and that may make you think seriously about what I'm going to tell you next:

1) A universal life insurance policy that was sold in 1998 showed illustrations with then-current assumptions that the policy cash value would earn around 7.5% for the next 30 years. For the last five to seven years, this level has not been reached. That equals a drastically lower cash value than was forecast, meaning the policy has less value than whoever holds it thinks it does.

2) Permanent life insurance policies are not as permanent as you might think, and policies sold to us Boomers will, on average, expire or become underfunded when we reach the age of 81 or younger (pretty much right when you need that equity and are approaching death). This is an average, and it is not true of all policies, but the risk is there.

If you wait, like Tom did, until you get that letter from your insurance company telling you your insurance policy is underfunded, you're going to have a problem. There are things that can be done, but you'll already have lost a lot of money. So why wait? This entire chapter has been leading up to one very, very important thing.

You need to review your insurance policy.

If Tom's policy had been reviewed earlier, things could have been changed to prevent his being in the situation that he's in right now. And the same goes for you. There is a critical need (and I'm not overstating this!) for life insurance policies to be reviewed. It doesn't matter what kind of policy you have, though universal life and universal variable policies are especially in need of review. You need to know what is happening with your life insurance. Is it performing as well as it should? Are there better options? Are you at risk of its expiring before you do? Given the recent history of underperformance in the life insurance industry (particularly with the kinds of policies Boomers have most often), it's absolutely imperative that you find out where your policy sits. And that means reviewing it.

Now, you might find out that everything's fine, and you've got nothing to worry about. And that's great. But you might find out that there's a problem, and that it's fixable, before it's too late. Think about it this way: do you want to take your car to the garage when it starts making that funny knocking sound? Maybe pay the mechanic to tell you there's nothing wrong. Maybe pay the mechanic to fix a small problem. Or do you want to wait until the car explodes as you're driving down the highway, leaving you with a far bigger problem (and a more expensive one too)?

Hopefully, we're all on the same page now. Your life insurance needs to be reviewed. So how do we go about that? Okay, you could review it yourself. That's a good start. I wouldn't really recommend that, though. We've already found out how complicated the insurance market can be. Chances are, the agent who sold you this policy has moved on or is no longer with the company. Calling your insurance company on the 800 number is unlikely to be of much help when it comes to reviewing your policy, because you'd get either a call center worker who can't answer many of your questions, or an insurance agent who wants to sell you a new policy. You might not need a new policy, though. So it would probably take you far longer than you'd like, and far too much energy, to decipher your policy and find out what's happening to it.

That leaves us with the professionals. Which, of course, is exactly who Tom turned to when he was in trouble. But with so many financial professionals out there, who are you supposed to go to when you want to review your life insurance policy? That's an excellent question, and one that we're going to answer in the next chapter. Let's find out who might be able to help you out....

Part Three
How to Find the Best Professional to Help You

Hopefully, by this point, you're pretty convinced that your life insurance policy needs to be reviewed. But now we run into a problem. It seems like there are a lot of people around who want to help you with your money these days. In fact, if you put together all those letters that financial guys put after their names, I'm pretty sure you'd get a whole can of alphabet soup. With so many people anxious to help you (and, not incidentally, anxious to get paid for doing so in most cases), who exactly are you supposed to go to?

Suitability vs. Fiduciary Standard

Before we get into the ins and outs of different professions, there's a couple of pieces of financial jargon that you need to be familiar with, since they're important phrases. Most financial professionals are held to a standard (a legal requirement they must meet when giving you advice). This is to stop unscrupulous people from giving you deliberately bad advice. You're paying a guy to give you advice, and in many cases he's getting paid whatever happens, so why should it matter to him whether the advice he gives you is in your best interests or not? Fortunately, the law protects you in this area by setting standards for those financial guys. There are two common standards: suitability and fiduciary. So what's the difference?

If a professional is held to a fiduciary standard, it means that legally they must give you advice that is in your best interests. If a professional is held to a suitability standard, it means that legally they don't necessarily need to give you advice that's in your *best interest*, but they must give you advice that is suitable for your financial status and goals. That might seem like a small difference, but it's actually quite big.

Let's look at a quick example. There are three policies on the table: policy A is perfect for your needs, policy B is okay for your needs but will earn the agent a lot more money, and policy C doesn't fit your needs at all. Nobody who meets either standard is allowed to recommend policy C to you. Someone who is held to a fiduciary standard MUST recommend policy A to you. Someone who is held to a suitability standard can recommend policy A OR policy B to you (and, depending on who they work for, may recommend policy B, since it meets the legal letter of the law AND earns more money, even though it's not so great for you).

If you're looking for the BEST advice, then you'll probably agree that you're looking for a professional who's held to a fiduciary standard, right? Keep those standards in mind, because you're going to be seeing them again....

An Insurance Agent is Where I Find Life Insurance, Right?

Probably most people's first thought if they're looking at anything to do with life insurance is to hit up their life insurance agent. After all, that's probably where you got your policy in the first place. We'll discuss in a little while whether or not that's a good option. However, as I said, there are plenty of people out there who may be willing to help you.

There are really five main choices, or five main groups of people, most people turn to. Let's take a look at them and find out what their pros and cons are. Ready for some alphabet soup? Then let's go....

1. Your Insurance Agent

All right, let's start with insurance agents, since that's where most of us would think to go initially. There are two kinds of insurance agents, captive agents and independent agents. Each has its own good and bad points, though in the end they do share a common problem. But we'll take each one separately to start off with.

A Captive Agent

Okay, a captive agent might sound like something from a James Bond story, but what this really means is an insurance agent who primarily works for one insurance company. Many will say that they represent other companies, but they still are sort of obliged to push their primary company policy. After all, that's who they work for! Already we have a problem here, as, obviously, since the guy works for one insurer, his job is to sell policies from that company. If you already know you want to be with this company, then that's not a bad thing, but it does mean your choice of policies is going to be limited. Sure, your agent might say that he's looking out for your best interests, and he may really be doing so, but he's only going to be finding the best policy for you from the list of policies that his company sells.

And ... all insurance agents get a commission for selling you a policy. Going way back to the 1980s, when I was an insurance agent, we got a commission for selling a policy, but we also got renewal commissions, which meant we got paid commissions also for servicing those policies, for keeping the customers paying premiums. These days, commissions are almost always "frontloaded," meaning that agents get all their commission in the first year and little or nothing in the future. Once you've bought your policy, your insurance agent has been paid, and unless you buy another one, he won't get paid from you again. See how that works? It's how insurance companies make sure that their agents focus on selling policies rather than on servicing existing policies. Besides, the company has the 800 number for that! Hmmm. We'll come back to that in a second, so keep it in mind....

An Independent Agent

An independent agent is not contracted to just one company. He works with several insurance companies and can get with just about any insurance company in the country. So he can offer you a choice of different policies and probably is more likely to find a policy that suits you, simply because he has more to offer. This is good for you, because it saves you time. Not stuck on one company you really want to use? No problem. An independent agent is a one-stop shop, meaning you don't need to go to seven different companies and agents to compare them all.

Not only that, but an independent agent can also move you around between companies if that happens to be the best thing for you. Cool, right? But remember, an independent agent still gets a commission for selling you a policy.

The Problem with Both

If you're buying an insurance policy, these are your two choices of agent. But we're not necessarily talking about buying a new policy; we're talking about reviewing and possibly tweaking your existing policy. And that's where the problem with insurance agents comes in. Insurance agents are paid to sell you policies! That's a bit of a conflict of interest if you're looking for an honest and unbiased review of your existing policy, right? What do you think the chances are of an insurance agent's recommending a new policy to you during a review? Fairly high, since that's how they get paid. What are the chances that he would be willing to spend a few hours helping you understand and tweak your existing policy for free? Not likely! Also, remember those standards? Insurance agents are only held to a standard of suitability, NOT a fiduciary standard. And while a good agent will provide as much service as possible, she does have a limit.

Bottom line here is that an insurance agent might be able to give you a little advice, and legally they're not allowed to charge for it. But (there's always a but!) insurance agents don't tend to know much about investment products or about planning, except when it comes to that sales pitch. And given that they make their bread and butter by selling new policies, it might not be an unbiased insurance policy review. Plus, they're not required to give you the best advice (fiduciary standard), only good advice (standard of suitability). Thinking twice about asking your insurance agent for a review? Not to worry; we've still got four other options!

2. An Investment Advisor Registered Rep

Okay, then, so what about another choice? We're generally talking about universal life and variable universal life policies, since those are what most of us Boomers are likely to have. Universal policies contain an investment part, and that investment is what makes you money, so why not turn to an investment advisor? After all, he deals with investments every day, right? Most investment advisor registered reps are someone who is registered to a broker dealer, names you might be familiar with like: Merrill Lynch, Wachovia, Bank of America, Edward Jones, or even an independent broker dealer for an insurance company. These guys should know all about investment stuff, shouldn't they? But ... (told you there's always a but) there are a few issues with these guys when it comes to insurance.

- Just like a captive insurance agent, a registered rep can only give you advice about his company's products. He is, after all, an employee of that company.

- The company decides which investment products an investment advisor can advise you on, so you might not hear about all the options.

- All investment advisor registered reps, in reality, sell investments rather than insurance, which can be a conflict of interest (since an investment advisor might be more likely to steer you towards investing money in pure investments rather than in insurance investments).

- Investment advisors in many cases have minimum account limits that they deal with, often in the million-dollar range, and won't deal with less money than that.

- An investment advisor might be earning a commission to sell certain kinds of products, such as mutual funds or universal variable insurance products, which gives you the same problem as you have with an insurance agent: he's likely to want you to buy new policies, rather than to work with your old one.

- Many investment advisors don't have the appropriate license they need to give advice (they concentrate more on selling) ... and then refer you to their "in-house specialist" to help you, who is a licenced insurance agent. And now you are back to the same situation as with other insurance agents.

- Again, investment advisor registered reps are held to that standard of suitability, NOT a fiduciary standard.

Whew. That's quite a list of negatives there. Sure you want to ask an investment advisor registered rep for help? Probably not, right? And I wouldn't blame you. So what about someone a little friendlier, someone you're familiar with?

3. Your CPA

A CPA is a certified public accountant. He's probably the guy you see once a year to take care of your taxes. "Accountant" means he deals with money, so he might be someone you think about going to for advice on your life insurance policy. Plus, you already know him and trust him to take care of your taxes, which can make this an appealing port of call.

There's a problem here, though. Your CPA is essentially a tax advisor, and that means he's a historian. He looks backwards at your finances, seeing what's already been done and then (hopefully, if he's good) figuring out a way for you to pay the least amount of taxes possible. All of this means that he doesn't specialise in looking at the future, looking at what will or could happen; he looks at what has already happened. So he's probably not going to be the best bet for reviewing your insurance policy.

Not only that, but most CPAs aren't licensed to give insurance or investment advice anyway. Some CPAs have an AICPA designation of PFS (personal financial specialist, and our alphabet soup can is filling up...), which means that they have higher training and more knowledge about investments and financial planning. But even these guys are unlikely to give you insurance advice, because it's not an area they're familiar with, and in some cases because licensing or regulatory restrictions forbid them from doing so.

Okay, then, your CPA isn't going to be able to help you on this one. He's your taxes and accounting guy, but not a great bet for an insurance policy review.

4. Your Friends and Family

Your friends and family are not a profession, and I did think about leaving them off this list. But that would be unrealistic. The truth is that many of us do turn to our friends and family when we're looking for advice. And, in many cases, this is a good thing. In financial issues, though, it's probably not. That's quite simply because, chances are, your friends and family aren't financial professionals who really understand the market. They do want the best thing for you, of course, but without understanding the insurance market and the financial market, they're not really well placed to give you solid advice. They know what has worked for them, or maybe what they've seen on TV (or read in a book!), but that's not necessarily the best advice for your situation. By all means, talk to your family about financial matters if you feel comfortable doing so, but you're going to be a lot better off taking financial advice from someone who understands the market and is educated and trained to give you the advice that you need in your circumstances.

5. An Independent RIA

You might be running out of hope of finding anyone to help you at this point! But enter the new kid on the block: the Independent RIA (Registered Investment Advisor). An Independent RIA is kind of a combination between an investment advisor and an insurance agent, with the good points of both, without any of the bad, and a little extra good stuff thrown into the mix too.

An Independent RIA will often have the letters ChFC (Chartered Financial Consultant) or CFP (Certified Financial Planner) after his name. Both of these designations mean years of studying, years of experience, and continuing education, as well as registration with the their resident state to do business. That means that an Independent RIA is knowledgeable and experienced in lots of different areas in the financial planning field: investments, law, taxes, pensions, estate planning, and, most importantly for you, insurance.

This is the new breed of financial professional, and one that most experts agree is the way of the future. So, what does an Independent RIA have to offer you?

- The Independent RIA takes all your financial information and makes a plan that's specifically for you. There are two kinds of RIA: fee-based (who work out a plan for you and then help you implement it) and fee-only (who just work out a plan for you; you'll need to go elsewhere for help in putting that plan into action). We'll come to the big differences between them in the next section.

- A RIA has hourly and annual fee models and can do the work for an agreed-upon nominal fee and advise you on what to do. Most RIAs usually have what is known as an "asset management fee structure" agreed to as a percent of the value of the account. All this means is that, in basic terms, the more money YOU make, the more money your RIA gets paid, which gives your RIA a vested interest in making a good financial plan for you so that he himself also makes more money. Plus, an Independent RIA will probably manage your investments for a lower fee than a registered rep or large company advisor would, because he needs to pay only himself; he doesn't have the overhead and corporate profits to answer to.

- You'll know how much you're paying up front. Strangely, in the financial industry, RIAs are the only professionals who tell you up front how much you're going to pay. Would you agree to use a plumber if he didn't tell you how much he charged? Of course you wouldn't. So this is a pretty big selling point for RIAs.

- Your RIA is a one-stop shop. He'll know all about your finances, your situation, and your history, and he'll be able to take everything into account when planning for you. That means you don't need to explain everything to five different people, and, of course, you get advice that is suitable for your whole financial situation, not just for one area.

- Reviews of your plan and situation (annual, semi-annual, quarterly, or even monthly) are all part of the service. That means that your financial plan is constantly being updated so that it's performing well and you're getting the results you want (and yes, that can include reviewing your insurance policies too!).

- Finally, and maybe most importantly, an Independent RIA is the only financial professional we've discussed who is held to a fiduciary standard. He MUST give you the best advice for you, every single time. That's a pretty big benefit if you remember what we talked about at the beginning of this chapter.

There's light at the end of the tunnel! With all these benefits, it looks like we might have found the professional who's going to help us with that whole insurance policy review. Out of the five different options we've discussed, it should be pretty obvious that the only one who's really in a position to not only give you advice, but to give you good advice without any conflict of interest (after all, a RIA isn't selling you anything; you're paying for his services, but we'll talk more about that in a moment), is an Independent RIA. There is one more little dilemma that we need to solve before you start finding your closest RIA, though. There are two kinds of Independent RIA, remember? So which should you go for?

But Financial Advisors Charge Fees!

All right, yes, financial advisors charge fees. ALL financial advisors charge fees, whether you see them up front or not. And to be fair, you're paying for a service, and if you're paying for a service, you want it to be a good one, right? We've already talked about why an Independent RIA is your best bet for getting solid advice, but with two payment plans on offer, what's going to be your best choice?

Both have pros and cons, and it sort of depends on what you're looking for, so let's go more in depth and check out the two options on offer.

An Independent Fee-Only RIA

So, our first option is a fee-only RIA. This is the guy who gives you advice only. There's no follow-up. He'll tell you what you need to do, but he won't do it for you. This is because he won't deal with products that pay a commission (such as insurance policies, for example). That means you get a plan, but it's going to be up to you to go to the appropriate place or person (say, your insurance company) to put that plan into action.

The intention behind fee-only RIAs is a good one: if someone gets a commission from a sale of a product (like an insurance policy), then his advice isn't 100% objective. He's influenced by the commission that he receives, or so the argument goes. For this reason, a fee-only RIA will usually (once he's got a plan for you) refer you to an associate who does deal with commission-based products.

All of that sounds very good, in theory. But (and here I'm drawing on years of business and insurance experience) it might not actually be that great in practice. Why? Well, in the business world, one hand washes the other. It's pretty rare for someone to do something for nothing. Most people would agree with that (as cynical as it might seem). Okay, your fee-only RIA isn't earning a commission, but he's recommending you to an associate who IS earning a commission. Why recommend you to that particular associate and not to another? That associate is not giving money to the fee-only RIA (that would be illegal), but there is some kind of mutually beneficial relationship there, whatever it may be. Is your fee-only RIA really completely objective? No, he's not. He has an interest in that referral that he's giving you.

This could be as simple as friendship. Say there are two possible insurance policies that the fee-only RIA thinks are great for you, but he plays golf with the guy who sells policy A and can't stand the guy who sells policy B. It's the way the world works. The reason I'm bringing this up is that, for some people, the main benefit of a fee-only RIA is that they're completely, 100% unbiased in their advice. But they're not. They can't be. It's impossible. If that's your reason for going with a fee-only RIA, then you might want to consider your decision again. Another problem with the fee-only is that their experience with commissionable products like insurance is only academic. They have studied it but not worked with it hands on. But there are other downsides to going fee-only as well.

That idea that you have to implement the fee-only RIA's plan yourself might sound like kind of a pain in the behind, and, to be blunt, it is. It means more work for you, of course. But there's also a fair chance that you could be spending money on nothing. Not that the fee-only RIA's advice is good for nothing—it's not. He's going to be giving you great advice. But that advice (and the money you're going to pay for it) will be worth nothing unless you put his plan into action. Unfortunately, many people don't. In fact, *Financial Planner Magazine* recently stated that 80% of financial plans are not implemented.

Finally, chances are that you're not going to be the ideal customer of a fee-only RIA. The fee-only RIA's ideal customer is someone who's got a lot of money and who already has a network of financial advisors. Say, a guy who's got millions and already has a CPA, a tax attorney, an estate planner, an independent insurance agent, etc. In these cases, the fee-only RIA acts as kind of a foreman, coming up with the big plan and then giving each of these other professionals instructions for what to do in their area of specialization. The team quarterback, so to speak.

Does all of this mean that you shouldn't use a fee-only RIA? Well, that kind of depends on you. You'll pay less money for the service, since the fee-only RIA does less work for you. You'll get a solid financial plan that will help you. But are you willing to put the extra work in to implement that plan? Or, alternatively, are you willing to implement that plan and then pay a management fee so that someone else can keep an eye on things for you?

In some cases, this might be the best option, but in many, it's not. Let's face it: most of us want to forget all about this stuff and get on with our lives. One of the problems we discussed in the second chapter was that the reason our life insurance policies are at risk is because we thought we could sign them and forget them. If you're a sign-it-and-forget-it kind of customer, then a fee-only RIA probably isn't going to be for you. Let's check out our other option.

A Fee-Based RIA

A fee-based RIA is going to not only come up for a plan for you, but he's also going to put that plan into action and make sure that everything runs smoothly and goes, well, as planned. That means less stress (and less work) for you, which is obviously a good thing. Are there any negative sides to using a fee-based RIA? Not really.

Some would argue that because a fee-based RIA can work with commission products (like life insurance), he must be biased. I've already argued above that a fee-only RIA is also biased. And don't forget, that "asset management fee structure" means that the more money you make, the more money your RIA makes. So it's in his own best interest to help you use the best-performing product. AND he's held to a fiduciary standard, so he's legally required to give you the best advice anyway.

For most customers, a fee-based RIA is where it's at. It's going to be the simplest, most cost-effective, and best way to get the help that you need. This really is the best option for those who want great advice and who want to be assured that everything is being done to protect their financial interests.

Alphabet Soup

Sometime back in the late 1980s or so, *Forbes* magazine had an issue with a picture of a chimpanzee on the cover wearing a suit, and the headline "Anybody Can be a Financial Advisor." As much as it pains me to say, this is still somewhat true. We've talked about financial professionals above, those who are highly trained and are qualified in their field. But there are plenty of financial "advisors" out there with other letters after their names, so many that even I've forgotten what some of those letters stand for. So, a word of warning: unless you do your research, you have no idea what you're getting. Some financial designations like CFP and those from the American College take real study, months or years of commitment, and cost some real tuition fees. Others take a couple of hours or days and an open-book test. Whom do you want financial advice from? I'm guessing it's the guy who has devoted a large portion of his life to getting the education he needs to give you that advice, and staying current on products, laws, and services. So you might not want to be tempted into taking advice from the others (even if, in some cases, they promise to help you at a lower cost). Stick with the professionals! And, obviously, if the offer says "no charge," well, a brief, initial consultation to look at the situation and get an idea of what you need is standard. But to do all the work for free? You had better ask how he gets paid and get something in writing; otherwise, you might just get sold something.

In Closing

Insurance is a complicated business. I should know—I've spent over 30 years working in the industry. But I hope that I've given you a fair idea of your insurance options and what you need to be doing. My point in this book was really to convince you that you NEED to have your insurance policy reviewed. Why? Quite simply because I hate seeing people being taken advantage of. I've seen clients in severe financial distress because of an underfunded insurance policy, a policy that they were counting on to take care of them in their retirement, or to be their legacy to their children. And I want to stop this from happening. It's not fair, and it's preventable. Getting the right professional help, getting that policy reviewed, will protect you. So please, go get it checked. You won't regret it.

Summary

Before I go, I'd like to give you a quick summary of everything we've talked about, something that you might like to read again in a few days, just to keep things fresh in your mind. For me, this is such an important issue that I really do think it deserves consideration. It's also a complicated issue, though, so consider this your cheat sheet!

Part One

In part one, we talked about the different kinds of life insurance policies that are available. There are two basic kinds of life insurance: **Term Insurance** and **Permanent Insurance.** Term insurance is only for a limited period (maybe 20 years) and has no **Cash Value**, while permanent insurance is designed to protect you for your entire life. And, generally, it does have cash value.

There are also different kinds of permanent insurance, which we divide into two groups: **Whole Life** and **Universal Life.** With whole life policies, think guarantees—guaranteed cash value, a guaranteed death benefit, and the premium is guaranteed never to change. Monthly (or yearly) premiums in a whole life policy remain the same for as long as you keep the policy. Permanent policies have loan and/or withdrawal provisions. In a **Mutual Whole Life** policy, or Par or participating whole life, the company is owned by the people who own the policies, while in a **Stock Whole Life** policy, or non-participating or Non-Par whole life, the company is traded on the stock market and is owned by investors. Thus, mutual company whole life policies receive tax-free dividends that are usually credited to the cash value and increase the death benefit. Stock companies pay dividends to stockholders: i.e., investors.

What about those universal life policies? There are three kinds: traditional, variable, and fixed index or equity-indexed. Well, they give more flexibility. With all three, you can change the amount of premiums you pay within limits; you can change your amount of coverage. But there's still that long-term savings portion of your policy. Most have surrender penalties for the first several years that reduce the cash value if you need to cash it in. As with all permanent policies, they all have favorable loan provisions, giving you access to the cash value without canceling the insurance. And, since some of the financial risk was shifted from the insurance company to the policyholder, the "target" premium is 30-40% less than traditional whole life. We Boomers saw this as a "good deal" given that we are always looking to get the most for the least.

A **Traditional Universal Life** policy has a guaranteed minimum rate of interest on the cash value and a current rate if it's higher than the minimum. Your cash value is not invested in the market and is guaranteed by the insurance company. These interest rates are determined by the investments held by the insurance company, generally high-grade bonds, mortgages, and other types of debt.

In a **Variable Universal Life** policy, that savings portion of your policy can be invested for you through the life insurance company. You might make more money this way, though you might also lose your principal since you are investing the cash value directly in the stock market and the policy performance depends on the stock market. They really need to be treated as an investment, since your cash value is in the market, but most agents sell the potential benefits and are not investment managers. These policies also have fairly high expenses and surrender penalties for the first several years, often for over 10 years.

In an **Indexed Universal Life** policy, the savings portion isn't invested per se; it's pegged to an index (usually the S&P 500, for example). If that index performs well, you earn more interest on the cash value. If it doesn't, you don't, but your cash value can't be reduced because of a stock market decline. This cash value is also guaranteed by the insurance company, as with the traditional and not with the variable. It's sort of the best of traditional and variable. Interest rates for these policies are usually higher than traditional, but the minimum is 0%. The interest earned, if any, is then locked into the cash value.

Part Two

In part two, we looked at how, for various reasons, we Boomers are most likely to have some sort of universal life policy. Some folks have a whole life policy whose dividends have been reduced over the last few years. These policies were forecast to have large cash values based on the then-current interest rate and stock market projections, but as things turned out, they didn't meet expectations. The stock market didn't perform as well as expected (remember 2000-2001 and 2008-2009?), and interest rates have been close to 0% for a long time, so our life insurance policies haven't performed as well as the original projections, either.

Many of us were sold on the minimum premium payment on our life insurance policies to be "competitive," even though the actual cost of insuring you gets higher as you get older (since you're more of an insurance risk). This sales strategy would have been fine *IF* all the assumptions in that competitive illustration held, which they haven't. Some variable policies assumed the returns would stay at 12% forever! Obviously, that has not happened! Not even close! The extra cost of actually insuring you should be covered by all the money that the cash value is accumulating in your policy. But when your cash values aren't earning the expected interest or growth, the insurance companies begin getting the extra money needed to insure you by taking it from your cash value. This is underfunded and early on can be saved. However, after a while, this cash value runs down until it's almost zero. Once it reaches this critical stage, the insurance company will send a letter stating how much additional premium is needed to continue the policy, because **these policies are about to lapse with no benefit or value! The amount needed to salvage the policy at this point can be tremendous!**

Once your policy is in "critical" condition, you can decide between cancelling the policy and losing all the money you've paid into it, or paying the insurance company a big chunk of cash to keep the policy running.

Part two wasn't all bad news, though! We also talked about how, with the right help, you can stop this from happening. Reviewing your insurance policy on a regular basis will stop it from becoming critically underfunded. It will stop the problem before it starts! There are several options for making sure that you're getting the kind of financial security you need from your life insurance policy, and a good financial advisor will help you decide which is right for you.

Part Three

In part three, we looked at the five groups of people you might turn to for advice about your life insurance: insurance agents (both captive and independent), investment advisors, CPAs, friends and family, and Independent RIAs (both fee-based and fee-only). To recap what each of these people can do, let's go back to Tom for a minute. Imagine that Tom had discovered his life insurance problem a little earlier and wanted help. What would each of these people have told him?

Insurance Agents

It doesn't matter if the insurance agent Tom goes to is a captive agent (working for just one insurance company and selling policies only for that company) or an independent agent (working with many insurance companies). The chances are that Tom's going to walk out with a new policy. Insurance agents these days are focused on selling policies rather than on servicing existing policies, which means, if Tom takes his problem there, he's likely to be told to get a new life insurance policy. The problem with that is that he might not need a new policy! It's better to work with an existing policy wherever possible!

Investment Advisor Registered Reps

So maybe Tom heads to an investment advisor instead, someone who works for an investment company. The problem with this is that investment advisors deal with investments and may not know much about insurance at all. The most likely outcome of Tom's asking his investment advisor for help is that either the investment advisor refuses to help him (because he doesn't have the appropriate license to give advice), or Tom gets advice based on investments alone—not on life insurance investments. This is obviously far from ideal. Or maybe he is sold another life insurance policy like with the insurance agent. Most investment company reps get paid for selling products, and that often includes life insurance and certainly annuities (look for my upcoming book on annuities!).

CPAs

CPAs are accountants, so maybe Tom goes to see the guy who does his taxes for him to ask for help. A CPA looks at financial history, not financial predictions, which means already we have a problem. Tom wants to know what the best thing is to do for the future, which a CPA generally can't really help him with. However, the most likely outcome of Tom's going to his CPA is that his accountant says he can't give him any advice at all. And he will refer Tom to his life insurance agent associate. Most CPAs will decline to offer any advice in this issue, knowing that they know little about it, and in some cases because the law forbids them from giving advice at all.

Friends and Family

So maybe, instead, Tom heads to his brother-in-law Jack's house. Jack works at a bank, and he has made some great investments, so he seems like a good guy to talk to. Jack is happy to help out, and tells Tom what he's been doing with his own life insurance policy, which Tom thinks is pretty helpful. The problem? Well, Jack has different needs from Tom, for a start. But also, Jack knows only about his own policy, not about all the other different kinds, and he's certainly not educated in all the life insurance options. Jack's heart is in the right place, but he's not really in a position to give Tom advice about all his choices.

Independent RIAs

An Independent RIA (Registered Investment Advisor) is someone who is educated in lots of different areas of financial planning (including estate planning, retirement, and insurance). That means that he is a great person to help Tom out, since he can take all of

Tom's financial situation into account when looking at his life insurance policy. There are two options here. If Tom goes to a **Fee-Only RIA**, he will get all the advice he needs to make sure that his life insurance policy is going to do everything he needs, but he will only get a plan. If he goes to a **Fee-Based RIA**, he'll get not only that plan but also help in implementing it. Obviously, an Independent RIA is probably going to be Tom's best bet.

We also discussed in part three the difference between a **suitability standard** and a **fiduciary standard**. These are standards that financial professionals are held to when giving advice. If a professional is held to a suitability standard, they must give you advice that is suitable for your situation. If a professional is held to a fiduciary standard, they must give you the advice that is in your BEST interest. Independent RIAs are the only professionals we've discussed who are held to a fiduciary standard.

And there you have it—your quick cheat sheet to life insurance! If you get confused while talking to your advisor, or you forget why that life insurance review is necessary, this is your speedy recap of all you need to know.

Glossary

Asset: anything that has financial value.

Captive Insurance Agent: an insurance agent who works for one insurance company, and therefore only sells insurance policies from that company. Compare to **Independent Insurance Agent**.

Cash Value: the amount of money you have "saved up" in your insurance policy. You can borrow against this money, and in some cases withdraw it. Loans accrue interest as with other loans but do not require any qualification, as with other loans. The loan amount is held as collateral against the surrender value and death benefit. With some kinds of policies, your cash value will be invested; with others, it will simply earn interest. It is an asset. Only **Permanent Life Insurance** policies have cash value. Also referred to as "accumulation account," "accumulation value," "equity." Usually subject to surrender charges for as long as 15 years, or surrender penalties. Compare to **Face Value**.

CPA: Certified Public Accountant. A financial professional who deals mostly with your past financial records and tax issues.

CFP: Certified Financial Planner. A professional designation awarded by the College of Financial Planning, and considered by many to be the "gold standard" of education and practice standards in the financial services industry.

ChFC: Chartered Financial Consultant. Professional designation awarded by the American College. While debated within the industry, most consider equivalent to the CFP to be the highest degree of education and practice standards.

CLU: Chartered Life Underwriter. Professional designation awarded by the American College. Requires 10 college-level courses and 100-question proctored exam.

Face Value: the face value of an insurance policy is the amount of coverage it has. Also known as Death Benefit. If your beneficiaries receive $100,000 in the event of your death, your policy's face value is $100,000. Compare to **Cash Value**.

Financial Advisor: just about anyone in the financial services business! Includes: insurance agents/brokers, stockbrokers, annuity salesmen, mutual-fund salesmen, RIAs, bank employees, trust officers, CPAs.

Fee-Based Independent RIA: an Independent Registered Investment Advisor (RIA) who designs a financial plan for you for an agreed-upon fee and then helps you to implement that plan. See also **Independent RIA**. Compare to **Fee-Only Independent RIA**.

Fee-Only Independent RIA: an Independent Registered Investment Advisor (RIA) who designs a financial plan for an agreed-upon fee for you but does not help you to implement that plan. Fee-only will not accept any form of commission. See also **Independent RIA**. Compare to **Fee-Based Independent RIA**.

Fiduciary Standard: a legal practice standard that requires a financial professional to give you advice that is in your best interest given your financial situation. Compare to **Suitability Standard**.

Independent Insurance Agent: an insurance agent who is not employed by one insurance company, and can therefore compare and sell policies from many different insurance companies. Compare to **Captive Insurance Agent**.

Independent RIA: a financial professional who specializes in investment management for a fee. This often includes many areas of financial planning, such as pensions, taxes, law, and insurance, in addition to investments. Not employed by an insurance company or broker/dealer.

Indexed Universal Life Insurance: a universal life insurance policy whose cash value interest rate is pegged to a financial index (usually the S&P 500). The cash value of your policy will rise or not depending on how well that particular index is performing subject to different crediting strategies. See also **Universal Life Insurance**, **Variable Universal Life Insurance**, and **Cash Value**.

Insurance: unilateral contract that defines the conditions under which the insurance company will pay an amount of money to the owner.

Investment Advisor Registered Rep: a financial professional who specializes in investments and the stock market. Most (though not all) are employed by investment companies or broker/dealers such as Merrill Lynch, Edward Jones, or Wells Fargo. Often referred to as "wealth manager," "stock broker," "registered representative (of an investment company or broker/dealer)," or "registered rep." Primarily commission-based sales of financial products such as mutual funds, etc.

Mutual Whole Life Insurance: a kind of whole life insurance policy sold by a company that is not traded on the stock market. This means that the company is owned by the life insurance policyholders from the company. Many of these companies' permanent whole life products earn dividends that are not taxable to the policy owner. Also referred to as participating or Par whole life. Compare to **Stock Whole Life Insurance**. See also: **Whole Life Insurance**. Also see: **Participating Whole Life**, **Par Whole Life**.

Non-Participating Whole Life: a type of whole life issued by a stock insurance company. Few companies still issue these policies. The insurance company is usually one that is traded on a stock exchange such as the NY Stock exchange. These policies have guaranteed death benefits, guaranteed cash values, and premiums guaranteed for the life of the policy, but do not accrue dividends. Non-participating policies rarely have a cash value that is greater than the sum of the premiums. Compare to **Par Whole Life**, **Participating Whole Life.**

Participating Whole Life: a type of whole life insurance that receives dividends each year. The dividends are not guaranteed; however, most participating insurance companies have been paying dividends for several decades and some for even 100 years or more. Dividends are not subject to income tax as are dividends of stocks. Also known as: **Par Whole Life**.

Permanent Life Insurance: a kind of life insurance policy that is designed to protect you for your entire life. It usually has cash value. See: **Whole Life**, **Universal Life**, **Variable Universal Life**. Compare to **Term Life Insurance**. See also: **Cash Value**.

Premium: the amount that the policy owner pays to purchase the policy. There is no binding commitment for the owner to pay, as with debts and loans or tax. The premium can be stopped at any time with the only consequence of possibly cancelling the policy. See **Universal Life**, **Whole Life**.

RIA: Registered Investment Advisor. A professional licensed and registered with the SEC (Securities and Exchange Commission of the federal gov.) or the resident secretary of state to give advice on investments for a fee.

Stock Whole Life Insurance: a kind of whole life insurance policy sold by a company that is traded on the stock market. This means that the company is owned by investors. These companies are the leading issuers of the universal and variable universal life policy since the 1980s to compete with Par whole life. Compare to **Mutual Whole Life Insurance**. See also: **Whole Life Insurance**. Also see: **Non-Participating Whole Life**, **Non-Par Whole Life**.

Suitability Standard: a legal standard that requires a financial professional to give you advice and recommend products that are suitable for your financial situation (though not necessarily the BEST product or in your best interest). Compare to **Fiduciary Standard**.

Term Life Insurance: a kind of life insurance policy that is designed to run only for a limited period, generally 10, 20, or 30 years. It does not have cash value. Premiums are usually guaranteed for the entire term. May or may not be renewable at the end of the term. Usually convertible to a permanent life insurance product without a medical exam or other medical qualifications. Compare to **Permanent Life Insurance**. See also: **Cash Value**.

Underfunded: the term used when the cash value of your life insurance policy and the projected interest rates and future costs will cause the policy to lapse at an earlier age than the initial projections. Like a cancer of a permanent policy—if detected early, can be cured; if left untreated, can result in significant financial loss.

Universal Life Insurance: a kind of permanent life insurance designed for flexibility. Sold by stock insurance companies. You can change the amount of the premiums you pay or change the coverage amount. Different methods and arrangements to determine how interest is credited or invested. See also: **Variable Universal Life Insurance** and **Indexed Universal Life Insurance**. Compare to **Whole Life Insurance**.

Variable Universal Life Insurance: a kind of universal life insurance where the cash value of your policy is invested in "investment subaccounts." These are similar to mutual funds in their basic makeup, except that they cannot be purchased except through the purchase of the insurance policy, and there are no listings in the newspaper regarding the performance, as with mutual funds. All information is found in the policy prospectus.

Compare to **Indexed Universal Life Insurance**. See also: **Universal Life Insurance**.

Whole Life Insurance: think guarantees from an insurance company. A kind of permanent life insurance that has guaranteed cash value. That cash value is in the contract with the company and will increase according to the contract. Premiums remain guaranteed throughout the life of the insured, usually to age 95 or 100 or longer. The coverage amount is guaranteed by the insurance company. See also: **Mutual Whole Life Insurance** and **Stock Whole Life Insurance**. Compare to **Universal Life Insurance**.